tea
essence of the leaf

sara slavin and karl petzke

photography: karl petzke

art direction, styling: sara slavin

text: lessley berry

design: morla design

recipes, food styling: sandra cook

CHRONICLE BOOKS
SAN FRANCISCO

Photography © copyright by Karl Petzke
Book and Cover design: Morla Design

Printed in Hong Kong

Library of Congress
Cataloging-in-Publication Data:
Slavin, Sara.
Tea: essence of the leaf/
Sara Slavin and Karl Petzke;
photography, Karl Petzke;
art direction, styling, Sara Slavin;
text, Lessley Berry;
design, Morla Design;
recipes, food styling, Sandra Cook.
    p.   cm.
ISBN 0-8118-1632-X
1. Tea. 2. Cookery (Tea) I. Petzke,
Karl. II. Berry, Lessley. III. Title.
TX817.T3S55 1998
641.3'372–DC21
97-17999
CIP

Distributed in Canada by
Raincoast Books
8680 Cambie Street
Vancouver BC V6P 6M9
10 9 8 7 6 5 4 3 2 1

Chronicle Books
85 Second Street
San Francisco, CA 94105
Web Site: www.chronbooks.com

Author credits:

The Joy Luck Club, by Amy Tan,
copyright © 1989 by Amy Tan,
permission granted by G.P. Putnam's
Sons, a division of The Putnam
Publishing Group.

Remembrance of Things Past, by Marcel
Proust, translated by C. K. Scott
Moncrieff and Terence Kilmartin, trans-
lation copyright © 1981, permission
granted by Random House, Inc.

D.V., by Diana Vreeland, copyright
© 1984, permission granted by the
estate of Diana D. Vreeland and
George A. Plimpton.

Riding the Iron Rooster, by Paul
Theroux, copyright © 1988 by Cape Cod
Scriveners Company, permission granted
by The Putnam Publishing Group.

Baghdad Without a Map, by Tony
Horwitz, copyright © 1991, permission
granted by Dutton Signet, a division
of Penguin Books USA Inc.

2/24
Cookery
4

contents

acknowledgments

Brewing a cup of tea requires two simple elements: water and the tea leaf. Creating a book about tea requires many more ingredients, working in harmony. The authors of this book want to offer our deep gratitude to the following for their unceasing gifts of time, patience, and creativity.

Nion McEvoy, Christina Wilson, and Michael Carabetta of Chronicle Books for their continued support, guidance, and encouragement.

Jennifer Morla for yet again surpassing our expectations and imprinting this book with her vision, wit, and infinite creativity.

Lessley Berry for breathing life into this book through her lovely words, vast knowledge, and never-ending curiosity.

Sandra Cook for encouraging us, from the start, to pursue this subject. For always expanding her palette and our palates, and for taking the art of writing and styling recipes to new heights.

Gina Amador, Leonard Koren, and Tsunayo Kimizuka for generously contributing volumes of information and hours of time and support, sharing sources and resources invaluable to this book.

Mrs. Yusuko Matsui for opening the doors to her extraordinary tea house and her vast knowledge as teacher of the tea ceremony so that we could photograph and learn about this great and spiritual tradition.

Mustapha Abdedaim and the management of Mariage Frères, Paris, for allowing us to photograph their amazing collection of tea artifacts and memorabilia in their Museum of Tea.

Michael Spillane of The G.S. Haley Company, tea importers in Redwood City, CA, for inviting us to experience and photograph tea tasting.

The Republic of Tea for sharing their vast knowledge of tea and tea tasting.

Betty J. Shelton, proprietor of Chai of Larkspur, in Larkspur, CA, for allowing us to photograph her elegant Salon de Thé.

acknowledgments

Sara Fleming and the management of American Classic Tea Plantation in Charleston, SC, for sending us specimens of *Camellia sinensis.*

Pierre de Gastines of Paris for creating for us some of the most elegant tea cups we've seen.

Iris Fuller, Michael Potter, and the staff at Fillamento, San Francisco; Sue Fisher King and her staff at Sue Fisher King, San Francisco; and the owners and staff of Dandelion, San Francisco, for generously allowing us to use their beautiful tea props.

Mr. and Mrs. Kobara for introducing us to the tea ceremony.

Margot Rego for generously sewing our tea cozy.

Maria Vella of Bomarzo, San Francisco, for the beautiful tea roses.

Anne Culbertson of Morla Design for her critical eye, patience, and humor.

Allyson Levy for recipe development and testing.

Emily and Peter Luchetti, George Dolese, Marcus Brown, Larry Tiscornia, Jack Jensen, Vic Zauderer, Deborah Jones, Jenny Thomas, Christina Salas-Porras, Roy Fong of the Imperial Tea Court in San Francisco, Gretchen Mittwer of the Urasenke Foundation in Kyoto, Japan, Dana May Casperson, Madame Chew of La Maison de la Chine in Paris, and Nilus de Matran for their generosity and kindness to us throughout this project.

As always this is dedicated to Mark Steisel, Sybil Slavin, Kate Slavin, and Lillian Moss. ~ S.S.

For your never-ending support, my love to Mari, Georgiann Petzke and Alfred Petzke. ~ K.P.

1

gardens

simplicity

Tea. Thé. Cha. Chai. Whatever the name, wherever the place, whenever the time, the uncomplicated infusion of leaf in water awakens the body, refreshes the senses, and soothes the spirit. A Beijing mother starts her day by lighting the fire that heats the family kettle. A Bombay street vendor, anticipating the afternoon scurry, balances a tray of teetering glassfuls. A British lord ends his evening meal with sips from an heirloom cup.

Tea knows no boundaries. It is available everywhere and within the reach of everyone, costing just pennies per cup and requiring only hot water and the patience to linger a few minutes while the leaves impart their singular flavor. Next to water, tea is the world's most consumed beverage.

From Hangzhou to Zanzibar, more than seven hundred billion cups a year are prepared in one way or another—some the result of elaborate rituals, others the product of an unceremonious dunking of a store-bought tea bag. Some are sipped slowly with the kind of relish often reserved for a fine wine. Some are slurped hastily on the way from here to there. Many are enriched with milk, sweetened with sugar or honey, brightened with lemon, or enhanced with the bouquet of herbs and spices. The preparation is a matter of tradition and taste, the time spent a question of priorities, but the enjoyment of dry, wrinkled leaves steeped in water is universal.

Assam. Balasun. Berubeula. Bohea. Bombagalla. Chittagong. Chun Mee. Da Fang. Darjeeling. Dimbula. Dragon Well. Earl Grey. Emei Ruizi. English Breakfast. Fonghwang Tanchung. Formosa Oolong. Galaboda. Genmaicha. Goomtee. Gunpowder. Gyokuru. Hainan Black. Hojicha. Irish Breakfast. Keemun. Kooloo. Kukicha. Lan-Hsiang. Lapsang Souchong. Lichee Black. Lingyun White Down. Liu Xi. Makaibari. Maloon. Matcha. Millikthong. Mityana. Namring. Nilgiri. Nonaipara. Nunsuch. Nuwari Eliya. Pai Mu Tan. Panyang Congou. Pettiagalla. Pi Lo Chun. Piupao. Pouchong. Pu-erh. Puttabong. Ratnapura. Rose Congou. Rungagora. Russian Caravan. Sankar. Se Chung. Sencha. Shui Heien. Tencha. Theresia. Ti Kwan Yin. Tommagong. Tunxi Green. Uda Radella. Uva Highlands. Yin Zhen. Yingteh Black. Yulu. Yunnan.

The catalog of a fine tea importer is a litany of names infused with their own intrinsic poetry. Yet there is little rhyme or reason to the appellations. Many teas are named for the region or village from which they come: Yunnan, Darjeeling, Assam. Others, such as Gunpowder, derive their names from the appearance of the processed leaves. A few teas owe their appellations to myth: Ti Kwan Yin (Goddess of Mercy) is said to have been named by a poor farmer who tended a temple that bore a statue of this benevolent bodhisattva. As a token of her thanks, the goddess sent him a shoot of the young tea plant, and he went on to prosper from the harvest of its progeny.

As befits a beverage that has traveled from the East over millennia, sparked rebellions, and spawned fortunes, tea's origins are legendary. In China, its genesis is attributed to the Emperor Shen Nung, a health-conscious monarch who always took his water boiled since he believed this precaution promoted longevity. One day around 3000 B.C., so the story goes, he was enjoying a steaming refresher when a few leaves from a nearby bush blew into the imperial cup. The emperor's resulting sense of well-being led to regular sipping, and tea was born.

The Japanese legend traces the plant's beginnings to Prince Bodhidharma, a wandering monk and reformed womanizer rather possessed by guilt. After awakening from a dream of his previous conquests, he is purported to have torn off his eyelids in repentance. When he later returned to the fateful spot, he found in their place an unusual bush, the eating of whose leaves inspired his now-pious meditations.

In India, the same prince is said to have taken an atoning pilgrimage to China during which he vowed never to sleep. After five years, drowsiness overcame him, but a providential munching on the leaves of an unidentified tree enabled him to uphold his promise. Though the tales of Bodhidharma's tea tasting are fantastical, the prince did, in fact, travel to China and remains revered as the founder of Zen Buddhism.

green tea salad

Hot, sour, sweet, and salty all
are addressed in this salad from
Burma. Traditionally eaten at
the end of the meal, this makes
a great appetizer as well.

2 tablespoons green tea
1½ tablespoons fish sauce
2 tablespoons lemon juice
2 tablespoons soy sauce
1 tablespoon fresh ginger, shredded
¼ jalapeño chili, seeded
    and minced
2 garlic cloves, thinly sliced, fried
2 tablespoons shredded coconut,
    toasted
3 tablespoons peanuts, toasted,
    chopped
1 tablespoon sesame seeds, toasted
1 cup romaine lettuce, shredded
¼ cup tomato, chopped
2 lemon wedges

In a small bowl combine tea leaves, fish sauce, lemon juice, soy sauce, ginger, jalapeño, and garlic. Allow mixture to stand for 15 to 20 minutes. Mix in coconut, peanuts, and sesame seeds. Toss romaine and tomato together. When you are ready to serve, combine all ingredients in a medium size bowl, toss, and arrange on two plates. Serve with lemon wedges on the side. *2 servings.*

The plant that so inspired myth is *Camellia sinensis*, a Far East native related to the garden bloomer. Just two varieties account for most of the world's tea. The shorter, smaller-leafed China plant can survive a century or longer, but grows no more than fifteen feet high. The more prolific Assam can reach sixty feet, but has a life span of only about fifty years.

Both varieties favor a tropical to subtropical climate with sunny days and plenty of moisture. The cooler temperatures of high altitudes restrict growth and concentrate flavor, so many of the best teas come from mountainous regions such as India's Darjeeling, China's Yunnan, and Sri Lanka's Uva. Tea gardens, as the plantations are known, range from tiny plots to huge estates that cloak hillsides in a carpet of deep green. The branches are pruned to intensify growth and facilitate harvesting.

Most plucking of the leaves is by hand, when the flush, or new growth, appears. The timing and frequency of the flush, and therefore of the harvest, vary with the climate. Women do most of the harvesting since their smaller hands are better suited to fine plucking, the picking of only the first two leaves and a bud that is the mark of a fine tea. Coarse plucking, reserved for teas of lesser quality, may include three or more leaves. From the garden, leaves are carried to the factory, often no more grand than a corrugated garden shed, where they are variously withered, fired, rolled, and fermented to become tea.

The East is where things begin, my mother
once told me, the direction from which the sun
rises, where the wind comes from.

t r a n s f o r m a t i o n s

Just as wine, champagne, and cognac are permutations of *Vitis vinifera*, black, green, and oolong teas are different expressions of *Camellia sinensis*. The key distinction between the three types of tea is oxidation, a reaction of the plant's enzymes to oxygen that is commonly referred to as fermentation. Black teas are fully fermented, oolongs are partially fermented, and green teas, as well as rare and expensive white teas, are not fermented at all.

Green teas, in fact, are but a few steps removed from the wayward leaves that flavored Emperor Shen Nung's legendary first cup. Straight from the garden, the freshly picked leaves are quickly steamed or fired to deactivate the enzymes that would otherwise cause fermentation. Rendered soft and pliable by the heat, the leaves are then rolled, often by skilled hands, into characteristic shapes: snail-like spirals for Pi Lo Chun, eyebrow twists for Chun Mee, slender needles for Lingyun White Down, tiny pellets for Gunpowder. Finally, the tea is dried in mechanical dryers or hot pans to reduce moisture and thereby arrest any further effects of botanical chemistry.

For black teas, the process begins with withering. Leaves are spread in thin layers on racks or troughs and left in a warm environment anywhere from eight hours to an entire day. The leaves wilt naturally, losing their characteristic stiffness and as much as half of their weight. They are then rolled, which releases the enzymes that interact with the atmosphere to bring about fermentation. Next, the twisted leaves are placed in cool, humid rooms where they are spread on slabs in inch-thick blankets. As their natural juices react with the moist air, the layers heat up like a backyard compost pile, then cool gradually, in the process turning from yellow to red to dark brown.

The famed Formosa Oolong, often referred to as the champagne of teas, gets its sparkling, fruity flavor from a shortened withering—four to five hours—followed by a partial fermentation. When the outer edges of the leaves have changed to a greenish brown, the tea is fired to stop the reaction, then rolled and dried.

Whether green, black, or oolong, the finished tea is graded. The ubiquitous Orange Pekoe (pronounced PECK-oh) of tea-bag fame is a grade used in India and Sri Lanka, not a type of tea. Most is packed in foil-lined wooden chests and shipped to auctions in cities like Calcutta, Colombo, Djakarta, Mombasa, and Yokohama, as well as the European tea centers of Hamburg, Amsterdam, and London. There, highly trained brokers representing importers from around the world assess the latest crop for appearance and flavor, then place their bids. The auctions are subdued affairs, more gentlemanly politesse than horse-trader hullabaloo.

green tea and rose petal popsicles

These are clean and healthy alternative treats. You can make them with any tea.

3 cups water

1½ tablespoons green tea leaves
(about 3 tea bags)

¼ cup assorted organic small
rose petals

Bring the water to a boil and remove from heat. Pour over tea in a ceramic teapot. Fill popsicle molds loosely with rose petals. Steep tea for 5 minutes and strain into popsicle holders. Freeze in the freezer for 30 minutes, then place the wooden sticks in the center of the popsicle holders. (This is a good time to spread the petals throughout the mold evenly.) Freeze until solid and serve immediately.

6 popsicles.

Darjeeling, before dawn. A light rain mists the chilly mountain air, sloughing off memories of Calcutta's ragtag streets. This bungalow, an aerie at some 6,000 feet, was built to house tea farmers of the Raj. Their legacy endures in the waistcoat of the turbaned waiter who served last night's feast, in the deep green plants that cover the hillsides, in garden names like Castleton, Bloomfield, and Margaret's Hope.

Almost on time, the taxi arrives, its fringe-bedecked interior part personal shrine, part roving salon. Sputtering in protest, it climbs first to Tiger Hill. The tea wallah's warm offerings ward off the chill. Kanchenjunga and Everest show their peaks as low clouds paint the voluptuous hills below in a wash of gray. The crowd cheers the sunrise; the descent to the workaday world begins. The shrine-on-wheels jiggles its way downward toward the garden.

It is the season of the first flush, that most coveted of the region's harvests. Among the waist-high bushes, a cadre of brown-eyed women deftly pluck the jewels of each plant, their bangled wrists tinkling as they work. In the factory, a jangle of aromas reveals the intricacies of this highly prized tea. The taster prepares a cup. Muscat grapes from Sauternes, black currants from the British Isles, almonds from the Mediterranean: The flavors merge mellifluously here in a mountainous corner of India.

2

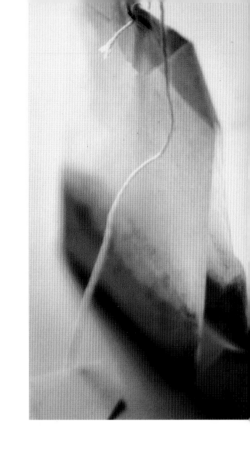

water

H$_2$O

Water is, of course, as essential to tea as the leaves themselves. Without those molecules of hydrogen and oxygen, there would be neither life nor tea—and the water itself makes a difference. Early Chinese tea masters are said to have had palates so sensitive, they could identify whether a cup was brewed with water from the edge of a river, from the more sprightly midstream, or from a well. Lu Yu, the first to chronicle tea in his eighth-century classic, the *Ch'a Ching*, espoused spring water as best, followed by river water, then well water. In Manhattan's early days, tea-loving Dutch settlers identified springs and installed pumps at points around the city specifically to ensure flavorsome brews.

Without doubt, freshness and purity count. The oxygen in water contributes to infusion; water that has languished in a hot water heater, household pipes, or a coffee-shop urn goes flat, loosing this essential element. Similarly, water can, quite literally, have the life boiled out of it. With regard to purity, the calcium, magnesium, or iron in hard water undermine tea's aroma and taste (some major brands adjust blends regionally to compensate), and may also cloud the brew or even form an unseemly film on the surface. Therefore, the careful connoisseur begins tea preparations with soft, fresh water and cuts the heat as soon as the kettle begins to boil.

SU DONG PO,
SUNG DYNASTY POET

Living water must be boiled with living fire,

I fetch deep clear water by the Fishing Rock

A big bucket saved the moon into a jar for spring,

A small scoop divided the stream into a bottle

for the evening.

accoutrements

Besides fresh water, Lu Yu's treatise prescribed twenty-four different implements essential for the proper preparation and enjoyment of tea. But today's tea fancier need not devote an entire cabinet to accoutrements: a teapot, an infuser or strainer, a cup, and a canister will suffice.

Teapots, of course, come in all shapes, sizes, and materials. The first were most likely stoneware from Yixing, and pots from the town are still prized for their particular affinity for tea. However, any unglazed ceramic pot should be reserved solely for tea since its porous walls will absorb, then impart, other flavors. Silver teapots, so essential to Victorian tea parties, conduct heat away from the tea, a drawback for which their singular sheen more than compensates. Glazed stoneware and porcelain are good choices, and glass affords an enticing view of that tempest in a teapot known as the agony of the leaves.

An infuser or strainer ensures a leaf-free cup. The former holds the leaves as they steep and may be a ceramic or glass sieve built into the pot, a metal acorn or wire-mesh ball, or a bag sewn of natural fibers. In lieu of an infuser, a bamboo, wire, or silver strainer will catch the leaves as the tea is poured.

The cup itself offers infinite variety, from delicate bone china to glass to sturdy ceramics—and everything in between. In China and Japan, a small, handleless cup is the preferred vessel (the first brought to Europe held only a few thimblefuls of liquid). In Russia and Morocco, a glass is more common. The handled teacup was an English innovation, an idea borrowed from the tankards used at the time for bracing hot toddies.

A tea caddy completes the necessary equipage. Time, light, humidity, and other aromas are tea's natural enemies. Buying in small quantities and storing each type separately in a tightly sealed, opaque container will prolong freshness and prevent flavors from mingling.

Those who like to linger over a pot may want to add a tea cozy to their paraphernalia. Usually knitted of wool or sewn of quilted fabric, you can choose from an assortment of whimsical or elegant shapes: a contented cat, an architectural landmark, an antique dome of monogrammed linen. Or perhaps a clock face, the hands pointing to four o'clock—the traditional hour for an afternoon pick-me-up. Whatever your pleasure, the brew will stay hot longer with this extra layer of insulation.

Within the lore of tea, the essentials of brewing a perfect pot are much discussed and frequently debated. In reading recipe after recipe, admonition after admonition, certain constants emerge.

Start with fresh water, as pure as possible. Since bottled mineral waters sit on grocery shelves and may contain their own disruptive flavors, filtered tap water is perhaps the best solution. Let it run freely for thirty seconds or so to clear stale water from the pipes.

The leaves need room to unfurl as they steep. An infuser must be large enough so as not to cramp their swelling, and should not impart any flavor of its own. In lieu of a pot with a built-in infuser, a natural-fiber bag or wire-mesh ball is the best choice.

Whether to warm the pot and whether its interior should be wet or dry is a matter of contention. In the end, it makes little difference. Certainly, the pot should not be cold, and preheating delicate porcelain with a rinse or bath of hot water is wise.

As to the quantity of tea, again there is no steadfast rule to guide the uninitiated. It is largely a matter of taste. A level teaspoon per cup is a good starting point; delicate green or white teas may require up to double that amount.

The ideal water temperature varies with the type of tea. For black and oolong teas, water should just reach the boiling point—

overboiling dulls the water and degrades the brew's flavor. To preserve the more delicate flavors of green and white teas, boiling water should be cooled to approximately 158 degrees Fahrenheit/ 70 degrees Celsius.

The ideal time to steep varies with the size of the leaf as well as the type of tea. Broken-leaf black and all green teas should steep for about three minutes; whole-leaf black and oolong teas for five to seven, depending upon their strength of flavor and personal preference. White teas need seven to fifteen minutes. Overbrewing leads to a bitter concoction: If tea must sit, remove the leaves and cover the pot with a cozy to keep warm.

To clean the pot, simply rinse with hot water; soap may leave a film that will spoil future brews. Placing a lump of sugar in the bottom of the pot and leaving the lid off will prevent a musty odor. Should tea go moldy in the pot, first rinse well, then insert a few curls of lemon zest, add boiling water, and let steep for twenty-four hours.

Warning: Tea does stain. If dribbles land on a prized tablecloth, rub any spots with lemon or hot, soapy water as soon as possible. On wool or silk, a recommended method is to dilute an egg yolk with warm water; rub lightly into the stain, and let dry.

black currant tea fruit soup

You can vary the fruits used in this light dessert soup. Berries would make a wonderful addition.

2½ cups water

1 cup sweet white wine

2 tablespoons black currant tea leaves

2 3-inch pieces of fresh lemongrass,
   cut in half and bruised

4 sprigs of thyme

pulp from 3 ripe passionfruits

2 mangos, seeded and diced

½ honeydew melon, diced

Chill four shallow soup bowls. Combine water and wine and heat until just below the boiling point. Remove from heat and stir in the tea; steep for 3 to 4 minutes. Strain the tea mixture into a medium size ceramic bowl. Add the lemongrass, thyme, and fruit. Chill in the refrigerator, stirring once after 15 minutes. Spoon into chilled soup bowls.

4 servings (makes 5 cups).

Bright. Fruity. Intense. Smooth. Toasty. Mellow. The tea taster's vocabulary echoes the sommelier's. Before a pound of tea reaches store shelves, it is tasted again and again. At the factory, the auction house, and the importer, professionals assess the dried and infused leaves for appearance and aroma, the infusion for color, brightness, and flavor. Mindful of the days when unscrupulous tea traders tampered with their product, governments in many importing countries employ tasters who have a pass at the brew. Like accomplished wine tasters, these experts can identify a tea's provenance without looking at a label.

Though most palates may never develop such sensitivity, tea tasting is an enjoyable pastime that enhances the appreciation of tea's subtleties. To mimic the professional's procedure, start with uniform white cups (experts use bowls, brewing the tea in lidded mugs equipped with a leaf-filtering serrated spout). Keep water temperature constant, as well as the quantity of water and tea (a teaspoon per cup). Align cups in a row, measure out tea, and add boiling water. When the water has cooled slightly, spoon up some of the infused leaf and inhale the aroma. Taste from the spoon, slurping energetically so the tea swishes across the entire palate. Try comparing four Darjeelings or four Ceylons, or taste a sample tea first, then try to distinguish it among four or five. Take notes, push the limits of language, and revel in tea's intricacies.

Soil, weather, time of harvest, and processing all affect a tea's flavor. Where a high-grown Ceylon from a single estate may be stellar one year, it may pale in comparison the next. Yet the everyday tea lover will never taste a vintage Ceylon since most store-bought teas, including gourmet offerings, are blends. These amalgams may include thirty teas, each painstakingly selected by the packager's tasters to produce a cup that is consistent with the company's style.

With all the natural phenomena and human wizardry wrapped up in a bag or tin, it is no wonder that purists disdain the addition of milk, sugar, honey, or lemon. The practice of doctoring tea with other flavorings no doubt sprang from a desire to mask the off taste of inferior shipments. The Chinese, after all, have preferred their own tea plain for centuries.

The Russians, to whom tea first came by way of overland camel caravans, added lemon slices, quite possibly to overcome a dusty taste the leaves picked up along the way. Those in the Near East suffused their caravan tea with sugar, the sweet crystals being a sign of wealth. The Dutch, the first to ship tea to Europe, added a splash of milk to soften the astringency of strong black teas; the British made the practice an institution. And everyone knows that a dollop of honey in tea can soothe a sore throat. The best rule of thumb for aspiring aficionados? Try it straight first, then see where your palate leads you.

mint tea cookies dipped in bitter-sweet chocolate

These delicate crispy cookies are made with peppermint tea. You could easily substitute spearmint, or try a little of both.

2 teaspoons brown sugar
½ cup (1 stick) unsalted butter, at room temperature
¾ cup sugar
1 large egg
1 egg yolk
1 teaspoon lemon juice
1½ teaspoons peppermint tea (the contents of one tea bag)
1½ cups all-purpose flour
4 ounces bittersweet chocolate

Combine the sugars and butter, beating until light and fluffy. Add the egg and egg yolk, lemon juice, and tea leaves. Beat until mixed in. Add the flour, beating until just blended. Gather dough into a ball, wrap in plastic and refrigerate for a half hour. Preheat oven to 400 degrees F. Lightly dust rolling surface. Roll out the dough to ⅛-inch thick. With a cookie cutter (about 2 inches in diameter), cut small circles, placing on parchment-lined baking sheets. Bake for about 10 minutes or until cookies begin to turn golden on the edges. When the cookies are done, melt the chocolate in a double boiler (or in a microwave for 3 minutes on defrost setting). Dip each cooled cookie into the chocolate. Place dipped cookies on waxed paper to harden chocolate.
Makes about 2 dozen cookies.

*Many years had elapsed during which nothing of Combray . . .
had any existence for me, when one day in winter, on
my return home, my mother, seeing that I was cold, offered
me some tea, a thing I did not ordinarily take. I declined at
first, and then, for no particular reason, changed my mind.
She sent for one of those squat, plump little cakes called
"petites madeleines," which look as though they had been
moulded in the fluted valve of a scallop shell. And soon,
mechanically, dispirited after a dreary day with the prospect
of a depressing morrow, I raised to my lips a spoonful of the
tea in which I had soaked a morsel of the cake. No sooner
had the warm liquid mixed with the crumbs touched my
palate than a shudder ran through me and I stopped, intent
upon the extraordinary thing that was happening to me.
An exquisite pleasure had invaded my senses, something
isolated, detached, with no suggestion of its origin. And at
once the vicissitudes of life had become indifferent to me,
its disasters innocuous, its brevity illusory—this new sensation having had on me the effect which love has of filling
me with a precious essence; or rather this essence was not in
me, it was me.*

The cup that delights and inspires also nurtures. In fact, tea was regarded as a medicine first. Enthusiasm for its flavor brought about the evolution from herbal prescription to everyday quaff. Over the years, tea chroniclers and entrepreneurs have extolled its virtues as a cure for everything from gout to rheumatism to the common cold. Today, science has shown that some of their claims are well-founded.

Studies indicate that tea's singular alchemy of caffeine, essential oils, and polyphenols, those substances often mistakenly referred to as tannins, aid digestion, foster healthy blood, and may even combat cancer. Caffeine, of which tea contains roughly 60 percent less than coffee, acts as a diuretic. Its stimulant powers activate the digestive tract in the same way they heighten brain power. Essential oils help emulsify fats, and polyphenols restrict the blood's absorption of cholesterol. The latter may also help prevent cancer.

And there may be some basis to assertions that tea eases the symptoms of the common cold and may even help stave off a bout. Green tea contains significant amounts of vitamin C, a perplexing phenomenon given that heat normally destroys this nutrient. All teas, but particularly green, also contain fluoride, which strengthens teeth and bones. While the casual sipper should not expect a cure-all, a fine cup is surely a guilt-free indulgence.

smoky tea
prawns

*A quick and unusual-flavored
salad, this is also very good served
over Chinese noodles.*

4 cups salad greens
1 tablespoon unsalted butter
1 clove garlic, minced
1 tablespoon orange zest
1 cup brewed Lapsang Souchong tea
1 tablespoon balsamic vinegar
1 tablespoon honey
1 tablespoon light soy sauce
20 large prawns, peeled and
    deveined

Divide salad greens evenly on four serving plates. In a large sauté pan melt butter over medium heat. As butter melts and begins to foam, add the garlic. Sauté garlic until fragrant and just beginning to turn golden. Add orange zest and stir quickly with garlic, about 15 seconds. Add tea, vinegar, honey, and soy sauce to pan and allow to come to a simmer. Add prawns and continue to cook another 3 to 3½ minutes, until prawns are opaque and firm. Serve prawns warm with sauce from pan over salad greens.

4 salad-size servings.

With all its beneficial properties, tea drinkers around the world have found creative uses for the withered leaf. No doubt more than a few of these practices come from old wives given to spinning dubious tales. A French calendar, for example, asserts that washing one's hair in tea for a week will transform the baldest of *têtes* into a Depardieuesque mane. In Sudan, a mother stuffs tea leaves into her young son's aching ear to fight off an infection. An English couple gives their spaniel a bowl of tea before bedtime, swearing that the brew, not their persistent grooming, accounts for his shiny coat.

Tea's astringency has long been valued by those two-legged creatures who yearn for a china-doll complexion: applying chilled tea refreshes the skin and cold tea bags soothe tired eyes. The cosmetic industry has not missed tea's beautifying benefits, and it is an ingredient in several popular potions.

The inventiveness of imbibers goes on. Sunbathing sippers soothe burns with tea-soaked compresses, and have been known to use tea's tinting abilities to impart a pre-holiday bronzing. Flea-market habitués let the same natural pigment turn age-yellowed linens a toasty ecru. The odor-sensitive take advantage of tea's absorptive powers, rubbing wet leaves into fishy frying pans or setting used tea bags in the fridge. And gardeners fertilize their prized plants with spent leaves. So think twice before tossing the liquor and leaves remaining in a pot.

Tea is very, very *important. The Orient discovered that thousands of years ago, and the English, having picked it up from the Orient centuries ago, perhaps overdo it a bit. But it's much too much undrunk in America. There's nothing healthier than tea!*

i t ' s   i n   t h e   l e a v e s

The beaded curtain rattles; the kettle begins to steam. Slowly, the kerchiefed woman pours, letting the leaves soak up possibilities. Sips of the dark brew bear a taste of the unexplored. She motions to swirl the leavings: three times, against the clock. Upend the cup, she signals, let it drain into the saucer. With an aura of knowingness, she turns it upright, setting the base within the leafy morass. As she peruses the leaves remaining in the cup, her words resonate with smoky overtones. The muddle of brownish matter speaks of a visitor tomorrow, whispers of a journey down the road, foretells of a love affair with someone as yet unknown.

iced green tea with wildflower honey

Dissolve the honey in warm water before serving it in a small creamer along with this fragrant cooler.

2 tablespoons green tea leaves

5 cups water

2 tablespoons wildflower honey

Place tea leaves in a teapot. Bring the water to a boil. Pour water over leaves. Allow to steep 5 minutes. Strain the leaves from tea. Allow tea to cool to room temperature before pouring over ice. Stir in desired amount of liquid honey.

tea drops

Little gems of tea flavor to serve after dinner, or drop a few into a warm cup of water and dissolve for a light, sweet instant tea.

1 cup water

5 bags of peach tea

2 cups of sugar

½ cup corn syrup

Place water and tea bags in a small, heavy-bottomed saucepan. Bring the water to a boil and allow to steep for 10 minutes. Remove the bags and return pan to heat. Bring to a low boil and add the sugar and corn syrup. Stir until all sugar dissolves. Bring temperature of tea mixture to 310 degrees F on a candy thermometer. Meanwhile, grease 2 nonstick cookie sheets. The mixture should have a heavy syrup consistency between 300 and 310 degrees F. Take care not to let the temperature go above 310 degrees F; it will caramelize. Work quickly with a teaspoon and drip poker-chip-sized drops of syrup onto the cookie sheet. Allow to cool for a half hour before plucking from the cookie sheet.

About 4 dozen candies.

While the almost infinite permutations of *Camellia sinensis* offer as much variety in flavor as a wine connoisseur's cellar, a multitude of other flora broadens the possibilities. Countless leaves, blossoms, barks, seeds, berries, and roots can either be steeped in hot water to make an infusion, also known as a tisane, or boiled in water, in which case the preparation is properly called a decoction. Their flavors—and often curative powers—have been valued since ancient times. The only caveat is to shun those plants, such as foxglove and mistletoe, that can be dangerous or even deadly.

A small herb patch in the garden produces an array of agreeable brews. Simply clip sprigs of rosemary, peppermint, spearmint, or sage, stuff them in a pot, add hot water, let the flavor unfold, and enjoy a steaming, homegrown libation. From the flower realm, infusions can be made with chamomile, hibiscus, lavender, orange blossoms, and rose petals. The garden-variety tea rose, in fact, was so named because its fragrance resembles the aroma of black tea. The dried hips of wild roses make a citrusy brew; so do the zests of lemons and oranges.

The spice rack, too, holds a wealth of exotic flavorings: cardamom, star anise, allspice, cloves, cinnamon sticks, peppercorns. Go ahead, experiment. Raid the cupboard and the garden, mix ingredients at will. Become your own master blender, savoring the aroma, then the flavor, of your own creations.

3

ceremony

As tea has traveled around the world, each country or region has cultivated its own traditions and rites surrounding the beverage. Some stem from necessity, some from practicality, others from spirituality.

In China, home of the first three millennia of tea history, tea was first used primarily as a medicine, then as an aid to meditation. For centuries it was mainly an upper-class indulgence, most notably a favorite beverage at imperial courts. Today, it is a household staple, as essential to daily life as rice, oil, salt, vinegar, and soy sauce. Guests are greeted with a cup of hot tea as a sign of welcome and respect. At meals, a teapot is placed on the table before the food, and again after the repast. At work, tea provides an uplifting break. On trains, conductors pass a steaming kettle so passengers can infuse their personal supplies.

Tea houses, popular gathering spots since the Ming dynasty, all but disappeared during the Cultural Revolution. Today, they thrive again in most every market village. On weekdays, community elders drop by with their caged birds as the last stop on their morning constitutionals. Come Sunday, families with children in tow transform the scene into a swarm of activity. Tea is everywhere, with no appointed hour or requisite ritual. It is pressed into bricks, wound into braids, and tied into chrysanthemum shapes, but mostly measured loose into the household pot.

PAUL THEROUX

RIDING THE IRON ROOSTER:
BY TRAIN THROUGH CHINA

Chinese trains could be bad. In twelve months of traveling—almost forty trains—I never saw one with a toilet that wasn't piggy. The loudspeakers plonked and nagged for eighteen hours a day—a hangover from the days of Maoist mottos. The conductors could be tyrants, and the feeding frenzy in the dining car was often not worth the trouble. But there were compensations—the kindly conductors, the occasional good meal, the comfortable berth, the luck of the draw; and, when all else failed, there was always a chubby thermos of hot water for making tea.

r o a s t e d
t e a - s t e a m e d
d u c k

This is a very streamlined version of the traditional three-day recipe. Sweet and smoky, it is an elegant entree served with green-onion rice and steamed Chinese long beans.

1 lemon

1 duck (about 5 pounds)

2 cups water

1½ tablespoons Lapsang Souchong
    tea leaves

½ cup blackberries

10 to 12 sprigs thyme

¼ cup soy sauce

2 tablespoons plum sauce

Cut 3 to 4 strips of lemon zest, each about 2 inches long. Cut the lemon in half and set it aside to rub the duck. Clean the duck by rinsing it under water and removing any fat pockets. Dry and rub with cut lemon. Place water, tea, and thyme in the bottom of a covered roaster pan. Place the duck on a rack in the roaster. Bring the water to a boil and cover. Steam the duck on the stovetop for 30 minutes. Meanwhile, preheat the oven to 450 degrees F. When the duck is finished steaming, remove it from the heat, lift out of the roasting pan, and set it on foil to rest. Strain the liquid from the pan and reserve. Rinse out roaster after it cools for a few minutes. Place the rack back in the roaster and roast the duck uncovered for 1 hour. While the duck is roasting, skim the fat off the pan drippings and place the drippings in a small saucepan to warm. Mix in soy sauce, plum sauce, blackberries, and lemon zest to simmer. The duck will be crispy and rich brown in color when done, and the legs should be reasonably tender. Slice duck and serve with warm sauce.

2 servings.

In the temple, incense hangs from heavy wooden beams in giant, skep-like spirals, the rich scent of sandalwood mingling with the perfume of time, of tranquillity. Filigrees of gold and crimson punctuate the dark, dense calm. A gong's resonating tones herald a passage—a signal understood only by the adept. The saffron-robed monks remain rapt in meditation, their gaze at once ethereal and earthly. But outside the sanctum, a cacophony of movement, color, and light assaults the senses. An omnipresent intensity propels a groundswell of polyglot humanity downward from the peak. Caught in the crowd, feeling out of step, a shop window beckons, proposing an escape. Golden-brown roast ducklings hang above a litter of luminous pastries, soft pillows of dough stamped with indecipherable characters and concealing unknown flavors. Through the door, a gentle, singsong hum pervades, punctuated by the subdued clatter of heavy porcelain. The table's worn visage attests to innumerable encounters, its blemishes somehow comforting. A nod here, a point there, gestures overcome language barriers: The waiter arrives bearing a steaming pot. Sinuous dragons dance faintly around its perimeter, their pirouettes having long ago succumbed to the strokes of a thousand hands. A sip of the warm, green brew revives. It sends thoughts homeward and carries them onward. To the afternoon, to tomorrow, to the next port of call.

While tea did not migrate from China to Japan until the eighth century A.D., the Japanese devised the ultimate ritual. The tea ceremony's highly codified mingling of religion, art, philosophy, and tea grew from a simpler rite that traveling Zen masters encountered in southern China, where the devout passed a bowl of tea as they gathered before an image of Bodhidharma.

Over time, enlightened monks, samurai warriors, and powerful shoguns left their imprint on this practice, transforming it into more elaborate rituals. In the sixteenth century, Sen Rikyu, a tea master of the era, brought order to the various styles, formalizing the particulars of the ceremony.

At its heart, the tea ceremony is simplicity itself, a blending of harmony with nature, respect for others, purity of spirit, and tranquillity of the soul. The tea house, or *sukiya,* is sparsely embellished; the motions of master and guests are minimal. Yet every detail is prescribed and becoming a master takes years of apprenticeship. For the Way of Tea, as it is known, is a path to enlightenment. There are two forms of the ceremony, a longer one that includes a meal, and a shorter one that involves just tea and a sweet, often formed in the shape of a flower or fruit to reflect the season. The tea is always *matcha,* a powdered green tea whipped to a froth with a bamboo whisk. The experience is all-encompassing, the antithesis of a quick cup grabbed in the rush of a workaday morning.

Tea spread to other Chinese neighbors as a means of barter. From the tenth century, caravans carried bales and bricks of tea across deserts and mountains to Mongolia and Tibet, where the stimulating currency was traded for wool, horses, musk, and herbal medicines. Both countries developed their own brewing styles, which survive to this day. Mongolians steep their tea with yak butter, then strain it and stir in milk and roasted grain. Tibetans season their tea with salt and churn it with milk and yak butter. The thick drink, almost a meal in itself, is often served with *tsamba,* a flat cake of barley or corn and buckwheat. As in China, tea symbolizes hospitality, and Tibetan monks consider it a sacred offering.

Farther south, India long had its native Assam variety of *Camellia sinensis* and natives of the region no doubt discovered its powers. But it was the arrival of British tea lovers and an accompanying contingent of entrepreneurial planters that established tea as India's national beverage. Today, tea wallahs hawk the brew from roadside stalls and impromptu benches. In railway stations, a teeming centerpiece of Indian life, tea is served in clay cups that are shattered after each use, thus ensuring cleanliness.

jasmine tea eggs

*These eggs require some planning,
but they are a delicious and unique
appetizer.*

6 eggs, hard-boiled

3 cups water

3 tablespoons jasmine tea leaves

2 tablespoons soy sauce

2 to 3 pieces of dried tangerine
    peel, pith removed

Tap the shells of the hard-boiled
eggs just enough to crack them.
Combine water, tea leaves, soy
sauce, and tangerine peel in a
medium-size pot over high heat.
When tea mixture begins to boil,
lower heat and place cracked eggs in
pot. Cover the pot and simmer for 3
hours. Remove from heat and allow
to sit at room temperature for 8
hours or overnight. Remove eggs
from liquid and chill for about 1
hour. Peel and slice before serving.
6 servings as an appetizer or snack.

The migration of tea northward into Russia began in earnest in the seventeenth century, when an ambassadorial gift enchanted the czar and the Nerchinsk Treaty, the first between the two countries, established a boundary and trade route with China. The journey was long and arduous, making tea an expensive luxury limited to the nobility and other persons of means. The completion of the Siberian Railway two centuries later was the great equalizer: Tea became an affordable libation embraced by all.

The invention of the samovar coincided with tea's spread to the masses. This brazier-style tea accoutrement may have been based on Mongolian hot pots, or northern Chinese may have used similar contraptions. Yet it became uniquely Russian and determined the Russian style of serving and drinking tea.

The samovar is essentially an urn, usually of copper or bronze, heated from below. The top of the urn cradles a pot of tea, which stays warm and grows stronger as the day goes on. The thirsty pour from the pot, then dilute the brew to the desired strength by adding hot water from the samovar's spigot. Glasses are used instead of cups, a custom that makes it easier to determine the optimal intensity. In general, the preference is for a strong brew, often sipped through a lump of sugar or taken with a spoonful of jam. Lemon, too, is a popular accompaniment, a habit Queen Victoria brought back to England.

Tea moved beyond Russia into the Near East as caravan routes pushed onward. Although Turkey is better known for its strong coffee, tea drinking is in fact more widespread. In samovar style, Turkish households are likely to have a two-level pot going all day, the bottom portion containing boiling water and the top a constantly strengthening brew. A glass is again the chosen vessel, and the tea is diluted with boiling water to suit the imbiber's taste. Tea is a daily essential, to the point that mothers have been known to assess a potential daughter-in-law's tea-making talents before sanctioning a son's marriage.

In Egypt, the government subsidizes tea's importation rather than risk riotous throngs. It is mostly low-grade dust from Sri Lanka or India, taken strong with plenty of sugar. Offering a glass of tea to visitors in the home is customary etiquette and tea houses, many equipped with charcoal-fired hookahs, are a center of masculine discourse.

Tea's foothold in Morocco came later, a result of enterprising British merchants who lost other markets during the Crimean War. Now fragrant mint tea, an infusion of green Gunpowder and mint leaves, accompanies meals and afternoon snacks of sweet pastries filled with nuts and drenched in honey. Making tea is a male province, and the shapely pot is held high above small glasses as the brew is poured, a practice that bathes the room with enticing scent.

So we began meeting instead at the sprawling Khan-el-Khalili bazaar, where we could take turns picking up the tab for sipping tea and smoking water pipes—and rarely spend more than two dollars. Our favorite haunt became Fishawy's, a back-alley teahouse that had been open twenty-four hours a day for two hundred years, without evidence of a single renovation. One-bladed fans clung precariously to the ceiling, looking as though they might descend at any moment to decapitate unwary patrons. Century-old dust coated the mirrors and the unflattering portraits of the café's former owners: portly men in Ottoman fezzes, perched on tiny burros. Rickety chairs and tables spilled into the alley, already crowded with peddlers selling papyrus, Korans, and hashish. It was there, stirring the coals atop three-foot-high hookahs, that we plotted and replotted Yousri's flight from Egypt, and talked long into the night about women.

thai shake

Enjoy Thai or your favorite full-bodied tea this way for a summer dessert or a pick-me-up on a warm afternoon. Curled lemongrass "straws," cut on a diagonal, make an unusual ice cream spoon or straw presentation.

2 cups water
1/3 cup Thai tea leaves
4 tablespoons vanilla ice cream

Bring the water to a boil. Remove from heat and stir in tea leaves. Allow to steep 10 minutes. Strain and chill in the freezer for 15 to 20 minutes. Place chilled tea and ice cream in blender and blend well. Pour into chilled glasses and serve immediately.
2 nine-ounce servings.

masala chai

This East Indian blend is spicy and soothing.

4 teaspoons whole coriander
1 star anise
2 cinnamon sticks, broken
1 teaspoon each: whole black peppercorns, allspice, cardamom pods, cloves, dried orange peel, and ground ginger
1/2 teaspoon ground nutmeg
3 quarts water
2 tablespoons Indian black tea leaves
1 tablespoon vanilla extract
Honey, milk, or cream to taste

In a small bowl combine coriander anise, cinnamon, peppercorns, allspice, cardamom, cloves, and orange peel. In a spice mill or coffee grinder, coarsely grind the spices. Mix in the ginger and nutmeg. Pour the water into a one gallon pot and add the spice mixture. Bring to a boil, cover, and simmer for 15 minutes. Add tea and vanilla and steep 3 to 5 minutes. Strain the liquid into a large pitcher. You may want to add honey, milk, or cream, or wait and offer these to your guests on the side. Tea can be served hot or chilled.
3 quarts.

Although the Dutch were the first to bring tea into Europe, the English made it their own. In the mid-1600s, the coffeehouses that had recently sprung up in London began to offer tea and the country has never been the same since. Although these establishments were exclusively male domains, women took up the tea habit at home. In 1717, Thomas Twining established the first of what has grown into an institution, the neighborhood tea room open to one and all. The tea garden, a later phenomenon where men and women sipped, nibbled, and listened to the strains of a full orchestra in the open air, has unfortunately gone by the wayside.

Anna, the Duchess of Bedford, initiated the custom of afternoon tea in the mid-nineteenth century. At the time, a large breakfast and then dinner at eight were the norm—servants were off duty between the two. To ease her late-afternoon hunger pangs, the Duchess ordered tea and cakes when the servants returned at five. The ritual persists, though modern lifestyles have pushed the hour up a notch for most of the population.

While afternoon tea may be as simple as a cup, almost always with milk, and a biscuit (or cookie), more elaborate spreads include both sweets and savories. The typical tea room might offer toasted crumpets, scones, and cucumber or egg-and-cress sandwiches, all satisfying accompaniments to that most ingrained of British expressions, "a nice cup of tea."

The fire crackles, spits, and hisses, a gregarious and steadfast companion. Outside, the bells in the village steeple join the birdsong, clanging once, twice, four times. As if on cue, the kettle begins a slow whine, building to a whistling crescendo. The full-bellied pot welcomes the warmth; the leaves wallow in the rejuvenating water. Steam rises from the cup, a cozier reflection of the mist that rolls across the moors. The brew is strong and bracing, endowed with all the spellbinding power of an Irish raconteur.

earl grey shortbread

These sweet, buttery shortbreads, filled with the essence of bergamot, turn a gray flannel color after baking.

½ cup butter, room temperature
¼ cup powdered sugar
¾ cup of flour, sifted
¼ cup cornstarch
1 tablespoon Earl Grey tea,
    finely ground

Preheat oven to 350 degrees F.
In a large bowl beat the butter and sugar until light. Mix in the flour, cornstarch, and tea and mix until dough begins to hold its shape. Do not overwork the dough. Pat dough into an 8 by 8 inch pan. Bake 55 minutes. Let cool completely before cutting into 2-inch squares.
16 individual shortbreads.

tea scones

Light and fluffy scones, perfect for jam.

1 teaspoon baking powder
1 teaspoon granulated sugar
1 cup all-purpose flour
½ cup milk
¼ teaspoon salt

Preheat oven to 425 degrees F. Mix the dry ingredients together, then add the milk. (Add a bit more milk at this point if batter is too dry to hold together well.) Place the mixture on a lightly floured surface and shape into a rough circle. With a very sharp knife, quickly cut wedges from scone dough. Place carefully on a baking sheet and put in oven. Bake 15 to 20 minutes.
8 scones.

Tea's introduction into France met with the sort of controversy that keeps Parisian cafés awash in lively conversation. It was sold first as a medicine, but many among the medical establishment denounced it not only as ineffective, but as downright unhealthy. Fashionable aristocrats of the time, fascinated with all things exotic, indulged nonetheless. The *medecins'* preference for herbal infusions, however, did have a lasting effect: Tisanes of chamomile, mint, linden *(tilleul)*, and verbena *(verveine)* continue to be popular afternoon or *après dîner* beverages.

On Paris streets and along the central squares of small villages, the *salon de thé* offers a less boisterous alternative to the ubiquitous café. No alcohol is served and, in true French fashion, the selection of teas and tisanes is typically of high quality. Earl Grey is a particular favorite, its perfume of bergamot especially appealing to the Gallic palate. Of course, a selection of tarts, clafoutis, and petit fours is also offered, frequently joined by American imports such as brownies and muffins. Whereas the café goer may well stand at the bar and knock back an *express* or *bière pression* in a matter of minutes, *salons de thé* are made for lingering. And they are without doubt *the* place to have tea in France, since most cafés are likely to proffer a pot of lukewarm water set beside a decidedly run-of-the-mill tea bag.

Were it not for a burdensome tax on tea imports from Mother England, Americans would most likely be as devoted to tea as their British counterparts. As it was, revolutionary zeal prompted a shift to coffee, and tea has never regained the foothold it once had. Even so, American ingenuity and zest for the new have left their mark on the chronology of tea.

In 1904, an English tea salesman named Richard Blechynden was dispatched to the St. Louis World's Fair with the mission of introducing black tea to green tea–loving Midwesterners. Soaring temperatures produced little interest in his brew, so he poured it over ice and the beverage was an immediate sensation. Four years later, Thomas Sullivan, a New York tea importer looking for ways to trim marketing costs, sewed his tea samples into little silk bags instead of using more expensive tins. Orders were better than ever, but customers expressed disappointment when their quantity shipments arrived packaged in tins. Sullivan soon obliged their requests for the convenient bags, switching the fabric from silk to less costly muslin, eventually to be replaced by paper.

Much later, these two innovations were combined in sun tea, iced tea made by steeping tea bags all day in room-temperature water. The American preference for tea served over ice is slowly changing as restaurants and specialty shops offer a growing selection of quality teas.

Shelves full of timeworn black tins line the walls, each marked with an exotic moniker hand-rendered in fanciful script. Those ahead in the queue seem to have deciphered the mysteries held within that parade of canisters, quickly placing their orders and marching off with a selection of shiny little bags tucked into their market baskets or briefcases. As the point of decision draws nearer, the untried becomes ever more enticing. "Dragon Well" simply sounds too captivating to resist.

recipe list

key to teas on pages 20-21

(ROW 1, LEFT TO RIGHT)
Pu-erh, Spring Plum, Violette,
Genmaicha

(ROW 2, LEFT TO RIGHT)
Perle du Thé au Jasmine, English
Breakfast, Gyokuru Karigane Cha,
Moroccan Mint

(ROW 3, LEFT TO RIGHT)
Darjeeling Badampton, South Africa
Thé Rouge, Black Tea Flower,
Bai Hao Cha

(ROW 4, LEFT TO RIGHT)
Montagne d'Or, Sencha, Kukicha,
Assam

equivalents

The exact equivalents in the
following tables have been rounded
for convenience.

1 teaspoon=5 ml.
1 tablespoon (3 teaspoons)=15 ml.
1 fluid ounce (2 tablespoons)=30 ml.
¼ cup=60 ml.
⅓ cup=80 ml.
1 cup=240 ml.
1 pint (2 cups)=480 ml.
1 quart (4 cups, 32 ounces)=960 ml.
1 gallon (4 quarts)=3.84 liters
1 ounce (by weight)=28 grams
1 pound=454 grams
2.2 pounds=1 kilogram
1 inch=2.5 centimeters

Oven Temperatures

F	C	GAS
250	120	½
300	150	2
350	180	4
400	200	6
450	230	8
500	260	10